MW00619045

DR. WANDA BOLTON DAVIS

THE
VICTORIOUS
LIFE

VOLUME 1

Mr. Graham
you are
Victorious !
Dr. Wanda

Copyright © 2019
Wanda Bolton Davis

All rights reserved. No part of this publication may be reproduced, stored in a retrieval system, or transmitted in any form or by any means—for example, electronic, photocopy, and recording—without the prior written permission of the publisher. The only exception is brief quotations in printed reviews.

Scriptures noted NIV are taken from the Holy Bible, New International Version®, NIV® Copyright ©1973, 1978, 1984, 2011 by Biblica, Inc.® Used by permission. All rights reserved worldwide.

Scriptures noted NKJV are taken from the New King James Version®. Copyright © 1982 by Thomas Nelson. Used by permission. All rights reserved.

Scriptures noted ESV are taken from The Holy Bible, English Standard Version. ESV® Text Edition: 2016. Copyright © 2001 by Crossway Bibles, a publishing ministry of Good News Publishers.

Scriptures noted KJV are taken from the Holy Bible, the King James Version, public domain.

Scriptures noted NLT are taken from the Holy Bible, New Living Translation, copyright © 1996, 2004, 2015 by Tyndale House Foundation. Used by permission of Tyndale House Publishers, Inc., Carol Stream, Illinois 60188. All rights reserved.

DEDICATION

To my father, Jimmie Bolton, a man of wisdom, who provided me a foundation and a living example of a Spirit-led life.

I love you!
Wanda (#1)

Special Thanks To

Kandis Davis Reese, Cover Designer

Nicole Staples, Artist

Linda Stubblefield, Editor

TABLE OF CONTENTS

~

~

1

EXCUSE ME!

~

When one of those at the table with him heard this, he
said to Jesus, "Blessed is the one who will eat at the feast
in the kingdom of God!" (Luke 14:15 NIV).

THE PARABLE IN Luke 14:15-23 tells the story of a man
preparing for a great banquet. He sent his servant to
invite the esteemed guests. One by one, they each gave an excuse as to why they could not attend. Let's take a look at their
excuses lest we find ourselves doing the same.

The first man excused himself because of responsibilities.
He said, "I have just bought a field, and I must go and see it."
The lesson here is that if we are not careful, we can allow responsibilities and obligations to become distractions that get in
the way of our relationship with God.

The second man excused himself because of riches. He re-
plied, "I have just bought five yoke of oxen, and I'm on my
way to try them out." In today's language, this man might say,
"I just bought five Rolls Royce cars, and I must go test drive
them." While there is nothing wrong with having wealth, we

must remember we are designated stewards of wealth in order to advance the kingdom of God. Our becoming consumed with the things of this world was never God's intention for His children.

The third man excused himself because of a relationship. He explained, "I just got married, so I can't come." Sounds like a good excuse, wouldn't you say? After all, God says, "Whatsoever God joins together, no man shall put asunder" (Mark 10:9). However, God makes it clear that our relationships should never become a deterrent or take precedent over our relationship with Him.

Jesus explains that as a result of the guests' multiple excuses, the man told the servant to go invite everyone. "Go out into the streets and alleys and bring the poor, the crippled, the blind, the lame. Go into the roads and country lanes," he said (Luke 14:23). In other words, whosoever will, let him come! That is what the kingdom of God looks like. Everyone is invited. You too have been invited to the banquet. Will you give excuses, or will you accept God's invitation into the kingdom of God?

QUESTIONS TO PONDER

1) What excuse(s) have you used that has/have prevented you from fully committing your life to Christ?

2) Who will you invite into the kingdom of God this week?

Journal the Journey

_____

_____

_____

_____

_____

_____

_____

_____

_____

_____

_____

_____

Affirmation

I will not allow responsibilities, riches, relationships or anything else to excuse me from fully committing my life to the Lord!

2

THE LORD REMEMBERS

~

"and the LORD remembered her" (I Samuel 1:19b NIV).

I F YOU HAVE ever felt forgotten, Hannah's story will bring great assurance that you are not alone. We can learn many lessons from her experience. Hannah teaches us the power of prayer as she cried out unto God for a son. Hannah's godly disposition can be seen as she was taunted and teased by Peninnah, her husband's other wife, because she could not bear children.

The inability for a woman to have children during Hannah's time brought about much shame and embarrassment to her. The norm within the marital relationship was for women to bear children. Because sons, in particular, were important for maintaining the father's lineage in ancient Israel, a wife was pressured to bear children. As a result, women who were barren were stigmatized.

Though Hannah may have been looked down upon from the culture's point of view, she shows us that true power is not found in a position in society, but in her posture before God. We observe Hannah's faith, as she did not take matters into her own hands; instead, she trusted God to accomplish His plan. The hand of God can be seen as He allowed Hannah's circumstance, hurt, and disappointment work to bring about His purposes and ultimate plan. Hannah's story truly demonstrates how God is to be glorified in the midst of challenging situations.

After seeing all the hurt, shame and disappointment that Hannah experienced, I Samuel 1:19b says, *"and the Lord remembered her."* That one statement is a reminder that God remembered everything that Hannah had suffered. God remembered her pain of not being able to bear children. God remembered how Peninnah provoked her. Even though Elkanah loved Hannah, God knew he didn't understand her pain. God recalled the prayer of promise she had prayed: if You will bless me with a son, I will give him back to you. The Lord remembered every trial and heartache that Hannah had encountered. Let Hannah's story encourage you today. Just as He remembered Hannah, He has also remembered you. God remembers your every hurt, your every disappointment, and every tear you have shed. God knows! God cares! And God remembers!

QUESTIONS TO PONDER

1) What painful situation are you (or someone you know) facing that has made you (or the person) feel alone and forgotten?

2) How does knowing that God knows, God cares, and God remembers make you feel? What steps will you take

to continuously remind yourself and others that God remembers you in the midst of your difficult situation?

JOURNAL THE JOURNEY

_____

_____

_____

_____

_____

_____

_____

_____

_____

_____

AFFIRMATION

I know that whatever I am facing, God has not forgotten me. God knows! God cares! And God remembers!

3

SERVE WELL

~

We always thank God for all of you and continually mention you in our prayers. ³We remember before our God and Father your work produced by faith, your labor prompted by love, and your endurance inspired by hope in our Lord Jesus Christ (1 Thessalonians 1:2-3 NIV).

THE RENOWNED RECORDING artist, Beverly Crawford, sings a song entitled, *Serve You Well.* In that song, she says, "Lord, give me wisdom so that that I might serve You well." Paul's words to the Thessalonians lead us to believe that they had served God well. After Paul writes telling them they were always in his prayers, he stated three important remembrances about the church of the Thessalonians.

First, he said he remembered their work produced by faith. Their steadfastness was a result of their belief in Christ.

Secondly, Paul remembered their labor prompted by love, for they demonstrated true Christian character.

Third, he remembered their endurance inspired by hope in Jesus Christ. Paul not only stressed their service unto the Lord, but he also mentioned the motivation for their service—faith, love and hope—the trinity of Christian virtues.

As Beverly Crawford sings, "I want to serve You well," we must ask ourselves, "Am I serving God well?" Let this song and Paul's words be a reminder to us that not only do we want to serve God, but most importantly, we want to serve Him well. May our good deeds be produced by our faith in Jesus Christ; may all that we do for others come from a heart of love; and may we endure and persevere in the faith because of our hope in Jesus Christ. Let us serve Him with the right motivation—with faith, love and hope in Jesus Christ. Then, and only then, will God say to us, "Servant, well done!"

Questions to Ponder

1) Paul commended the Thessalonians not only for their good works, but also the motivation behind their good works. What motivates you to do what you do?

2) Can God commend you for serving Him well? What steps will you take this week to serve God and others well from a place of faith, love and hope in Jesus Christ?

Journal the Journey

_____

_____

_____

_____

_____

_____

_____

_____

_____

_____

_____

_____

_____

AFFIRMATION

My heart is cleansed before God. I serve God and others from a place of faith, love and hope in Jesus Christ.

4

THE BIG EXCHANGE: YOUR WORRY FOR GOD'S PEACE

~

Do not be anxious about anything, but in every situation, by prayer and petition, with thanksgiving, present your request to God. ⁷And the peace of God, which transcends all understanding, will guard your hearts and your minds in Christ Jesus (Philippians 4:6-7 NIV).

HAVE YOU BEEN anxious lately? Has something been worrying you? The Bible tells you that you don't have to worry about anything. You can make your requests known to God in prayer and petition, with thanksgiving, and He will give you peace that surpasses all understanding. Paul gives us three components for communicating with God. First, Paul says we can communicate with God through prayer. Prayer is communicating with God by both speaking and listening to Him. Second, we can communicate with God through petitioning Him. In other words, we can make our needs and desires known to God, both for ourselves and for others. Lastly, we can communicate with God with thanksgiving. We are to talk to God and let our needs and desires be known to Him, while having an attitude of thankfulness and a grateful heart. Paul says in 1 Thessalonians 5:18 that we should be thankful in all things. We owe God our praise no matter what we may be facing. The result is peace that will transcend all comprehension. Paul does not promise that the situation will change immediately or at all. However, he says that God will give us peace that far surpasses any need, desire or concern we may have. We can all experience the big exchange when we do as the songwriter said: "Take your burdens to the Lord and leave them there." You can exchange your burdens for peace when you take them to the Lord in prayer.

QUESTIONS TO PONDER

1) Write down what you worry about.

2) For one week, commit to talk to God in prayer about your worries. Petition God for your needs. Thank God for His promises and provision. Receive God's peace for your situation.

JOURNAL THE JOURNEY

_____

_____

_____

_____

_____

_____

_____

_____

_____

_____

_____

AFFIRMATION

As I pray and petition God for my situation, I do so
with a grateful heart. I receive God's peace that is beyond anything I can imagine.

5

FOR THE SAKE
OF HIS GREAT NAME

~

For the sake of his great name the LORD *will not reject his people, because the* LORD *was pleased to make you his own* (I Samuel 12:22 NIV).

THE ABOVE VERSE was spoken by Samuel to the Israelites after they had rebelled against God's will by requesting a king to be led by a man like the other nations. Originally, the Jewish nation had no kings. God had told Moses at Mt. Sinai that if the Jews would follow and obey Him, they would have no need for a king. They would be "a kingdom of priests and a holy nation." Nevertheless, the people begged Samuel to appoint a king for them. Samuel reluctantly granted their request by appointing Saul as their king.

However, Saul's appointment did not come without grave consequences. When the people realized their mistake, they pleaded with Samuel to pray for them so that they would not die. Samuel responded by saying, *"For the sake of his great name the* LORD *will not reject his people, because the* LORD *was pleased to make you his own."*

Perhaps you are like the Israelites and you have also made a grave mistake; you have disobeyed God. Perhaps you feel that you have gone too far to come back to God. Although you may face some consequences for your choices, you can have the assurance that there is no such thing as getting too far away from God. If you have accepted Jesus as your Savior, God will NEVER reject you. Why? For the sake of His great name. His name will not allow Him to reject you. If He rejected you, He would not be faithful to His Word (Isaiah 55:11). God is pleased to make you His own. Nothing brings Him greater joy. He forgives and restores us—not because we deserve it, but for the sake of HIS GREAT NAME!

QUESTIONS TO PONDER

1) Do you carry guilt or regret about a decision you made that has caused you to wonder whether God has forgiven you?

2) Make a list of those decisions, then go back and draw a line through them. Next to each one, write, "I am forgiven for the sake of His Great Name!" AMEN!

JOURNAL THE JOURNEY

_____

_____

_____

_____

_____

_____

_____

_____

_____

_____

_____

_____

_____

AFFIRMATION

I am forgiven and restored for the sake of God's great
name. God is faithful to His Word!

6

VICTORY IN THE BATTLE

~

For our struggle is not against flesh and blood, but against the rulers, against the authorities, against the powers of this dark world and against the spiritual forces of evil in the heavenly realms. ¹³Therefore put on the full armor of God, so that when the day of evil comes, you may be able to stand your ground, and after you have done everything, to stand (Ephesians 6:12-13 NIV).

EVERY MORNING WHEN our eyes open and our feet hit the floor, we enter a battle. In reality, we are at war even in our sleep. The work of the Enemy is always all around us. I don't know about you, but at times I encounter situations when I don't always remember that I am engaged in spiritual warfare. When I am faced with a challenging situation, I find it so easy to take it personally or want to react in order to protect what feels threatened at the time. I'm sure you too have faced situations or people that have hurt you, offended you or just simply did you wrong.

Let me remind you that the war we are in is not one of flesh and blood. It's not the coworker, the friend, the stranger, the spouse, or even yourself at times. Rather, it is the spirit of the Enemy who is working to kill, steal and destroy. Although your problem may be manifested in the flesh, it does not have its origin from the flesh. It is a spiritual problem, and spiritual problems require spiritual solutions. Let us be reminded to stand firm and put on the whole armor of God, which is truth, righteousness, spiritual preparation, faith, salvation and the word of God; and don't forget prayer. These are the only tools that will give us victory in the battle.

QUESTIONS TO PONDER

1) What situation are you facing right now that you realize is a spiritual battle? How have you been trying to handle it?

2) What steps will you take this week to fight this battle in the spiritual realm rather than in flesh and blood (your own tactics)?

JOURNAL THE JOURNEY

_____

_____

_____

_____

_____

_____

_____

_____

_____

_____

_____

_____

_____

_____

AFFIRMATION

Today I resist the temptation to handle my situation in my own strength. I will engage my spiritual weapons wherewith God will fight the battle, and I will be victorious!

7

LIVE A LEGACY

~

For even the Son of Man did not come to be served, but to serve, and to give his life as a ransom for many (Mark 10:45 NIV).

I CAN RECALL my fifty-eighth birthday, which happened to fall on Memorial Day that year. As usual on that holiday, I cooked and invited over family and friends. However, what I had thought was going to be our usual Memorial Day family and friend gathering, ended up being a full-fledged birthday party in my honor! To my surprise and rather spontaneously, one of my family members initiated what ended up being a "string of tributes" to me.

One by one, family members and friends stood before me and shared how my life had impacted theirs. I was humbled and brought to tears as each of them shared how I had touched their life in some way. The event was sort of like attending my own funeral (Oh, my!) As I listened, I realized a consistent theme was appearing among all of them. Later, as I reflected upon the day, I realized how important it is to live the legacy you want to leave. We often speak of leaving a legacy; however, a legacy must first be lived and then left.

Jesus came to earth to do the will of the Father. He served others and was obedient to His Father. He did not come to earth and serve. He came to earth for the purpose of serving. In other words, His reason for coming was to serve. He lived the legacy He left.

Are you living the legacy you want to leave? What will people say about you when you are gone? Whatever we want that to be, let's start living it!

QUESTIONS TO PONDER

1) Jesus was our model for service. How do you serve God and others?

2) What do you want people to say about you when you die? Name three ways you are you living that out now.

JOURNAL THE JOURNEY

_____

_____

_____

_____

_____

_____

_____

_____

_____

_____

_____

_____

_____

_____

_____ ᎤᏑ

Affirmation

I am not only leaving a legacy,
but I am living a legacy of love and service.

8

LET GOD DIRECT YOUR PATH

~

Trust in the LORD with all thine heart; and lean not unto thine own understanding. ⁶In all thine ways acknowledge him, and he shall direct thy paths (Proverbs 3:5-6 KJV).

ARE YOU WRESTLING with a decision? Trying to figure out what to do? We have all been at that place of trying to discern God's will for our lives. Some of the questions which invade our mind could include:

- Which job should I accept?
- Where should I relocate?
- Which school should I attend?

While God's Word is very clear on some areas, not always does the Bible directly address our everyday decisions; yet we desire to be in His will. Proverbs 3:5-6 gives us wise counsel for those everyday decisions that sometimes fall into gray areas. We are instructed first to trust God wholeheartedly. This direction means to place total confidence, certainty and hope in God. It has often been said, "When you can't trace God, trust Him." In times of uncertainty, be reminded of God's character and who He is.

Second, we are not to rely on self-confidence for direction in life. Even when we are unsure about the next steps, we can be certain that God is with us every step of the way. Our security is not in ourselves, but in Christ alone.

Third, we are to seek God in everything—doing so assures that He will always guide us the right way. God knows everything. His path and plan for your life was formed even before you were (Jeremiah 29:11). Therefore, your uncertainty does not negate God's knowledge, guidance, direction and presence in your life. We may not have all the answers, but we can be assured that when we trust God and refuse to rely on ourselves, God will always lead us the right way—HIS WAY!

As you journey through life, believe God for new opportunities, new relationships, new ideas and new levels of faith!

QUESTIONS TO PONDER

1) With what decision in your life are you currently struggling?

2) Although you have the task of making the decision, how can you seek God and trust Him in it?

Journal the Journey

Affirmation

I trust God wholeheartedly in this decision. He will lead, guide and direct me. The outcome will work for my good and His glory.

9

STIR IT UP!

~

Wherefore I put thee in remembrance that thou stir up the gift of God, which is in thee by the putting on of my hands (2 Timothy 1:6 KJV).

ALL OF US can attest to the fact that we have had times when we have lost the excitement, fervor and fire in our Christian walk. Life has a way of bringing us to a place where we may wonder, *is it really worth it?* We've experienced demanding challenges, become discouraged and perhaps even felt like giving up. Sometimes we simply need to be in the company of the right person who will remind us that within us is something great, and most of all, Someone greater is within us, empowering us.

I want to encourage you, as the apostle Paul encouraged Timothy, to "stir up the gift of God which is inside you." Paul's words did not come to Timothy because Timothy had ceased to use his gifts; rather, Paul reminded him that his gifting was a continuous outpouring. Additionally, Paul was not implying that Timothy's gift came as result of the laying on of his hands. Laying on of hands has been a symbolic representation and affirmation of the gift that was instilled in Timothy by the Holy Spirit at the beginning of his ministry.

Like Paul, I want to encourage you to stir up the gift that God has placed in you. Fan the flames, and they will grow strong again. "How do I do that?" you might ask.

First, remember your faith. Go back to when you first believed. Remind yourself of the faithfulness of God. The prophet Jonah said, *"When my soul fainted within me, I remembered the LORD..."* (2:7 NKJV).

Second, rekindle the fire. Get with people in the place where you can grow, be sharpened and exercise your abilities.

Third, remain fearless and unashamed. Fear paralyzes your gift. "God has not given you the spirit of fear, but power, love and a sound mind" (2 Timothy 1:7). I urge you to remember the gift of God that is inside you; now stir it up and watch God work!

QUESTIONS TO PONDER

1) What gift has God given you that seems to be lying dormant or now seems to be as powerful as it once was?

2) Reflect on the time when you walked in your gifting with passion and power. Assess where you are. Have you gotten away from the place where you could grow and function in your gifting? What changes do you need to make in your life to rekindle the flames of your spiritual gift(s)?

Journal the Journey

_____

_____

_____

_____

_____

_____

_____

_____

_____

_____

_____

_____

Affirmation

Every day I walk in my spiritual gifting with passion
and power, fueled by the power of the Holy Spirit.

10

A Radical
Reorientation

~

Therefore, if anyone is in Christ, the new creation has come: The old has gone, the new is here! (2 Corinthians 5:17 NIV).

I LIKE TO watch the HGTV channel. Numerous shows focus on people who purchase old, dilapidated homes, and within a few weeks, these renovators overhaul, remodel and restore them into beautiful, luxurious living spaces. The before and after pictures render unbelievable transformations. The new home no longer looks the same; in fact, it isn't the same. Everything about it is different. Sometimes walls have been knocked out or moved; new appliances and furniture have been purchased; new flooring and cabinets have been installed. Everything is new!

Such a transformation is also seen in the apostle Paul's life. His Damascus-road experience brought about a radical reorientation in his life as he was transformed from Saul the persecutor to the praying, preaching and discipling Paul. His life was not only marked by his newfound ministry and his new profession—preaching and sharing the Gospel, but his life was also identified by what he no longer did—persecuting and hating Christians.

When we come to know Jesus during our own "Damascus-road experience," our life also becomes new. Our position in Christ is radically changed. We go from sinners on our way to hell, to being saved, redeemed and kingdom citizens. Additionally, some of our behaviors may be instantly changed like Paul's, and others may be more gradual as we grow in Christ. Nevertheless, through the Holy Spirit, a supernatural transformation takes place. Old things are passed away, and all things become new!

"What is new?" you ask, Your position in Christ, your perspective on life, your outcome in circumstances and your eternal destiny—EVERYTHING is made new!

QUESTIONS TO PONDER

1) Describe your life as a non-believer. What are some of the things you did, thought or said, etc.?

2) Describe your life now that you are in Christ. Has a radical reorientation taken place? If so, how? In what areas of your life does there remain the need for growth?

Journal the Journey

_____

_____

_____

_____

_____

_____

_____

_____

_____

_____

_____

Affirmation

I no longer _____. Now I _____
because I am a new creation in Christ.

11

IT WILL PAY OFF

~

Therefore, my beloved brethren, be ye stedfast, unmoveable, always abounding in the work of the Lord, forasmuch as ye know that your labour is not in vain in the Lord (1 Corinthians 15:58 KJV).

WHEN YOU INVEST money, interest accrues gradually—not overnight. Additionally, the more money you invest, combined with the longer amount of time you allow it to remain in the account, the greater the return.

The Christian life can be compared to investing. It's easy to accept Christ but walking with Him in long-term obedience is hard because you don't always see the tangible benefits nor receive the instant gratification. The reward sometimes appears to be reserved for the far-distant future. This reality, along with facing the spiritual warfare on a daily basis, can make the Christian life difficult, painful, tiring and discouraging.

But Paul gives some encouraging words, instructing us to be "steadfast, unmovable, always abounding in the work of the Lord." In other words, we are to be firm, unwavering, constant, unshaken, abundant and overflowing in our work for God because, "our labor is not in vain." Therefore, be reminded to keep making regular deposits of love, kindness, forgiveness, patience, obedience and righteousness because interest is accruing daily.

QUESTIONS TO PONDER

1) Do you ever tire in your service and faithfulness to God and others?

2) God promises that your labor is not in vain. What will you do to remain faithful until the end?

JOURNAL THE JOURNEY

_____

_____

_____

_____

_____

_____

_____

_____

_____

_____

_____

_____

_____

_____

_____

_____

AFFIRMATION

I am faithful and steadfast in my work for the Lord.

12

IDENTITY THEFT

~

The thief cometh not, but for to steal, and to kill, and to destroy: I am come that they might have life, and that they might have it more abundantly (John 10:10 KJV).

A FEW YEARS ago, a friend of mine found herself a victim of identity theft. Someone had stolen her personal information and had used it for their advantage. This unfortunate reality of today not only happens in the natural order of life, but also ensues spiritually.

One of the greatest strategies that Satan uses against God's children is to steal their knowledge and understanding of their identity in Christ so that he can use it to his advantage. When believers do not fully understand their identity in Christ, they fail to access the promises that God has provided in His Word. If, in the midst of your trial or adversity, Satan can make you forget who you are in Christ, he knows you will live life, feeling defeated and without the knowledge that you have already been given the victory. Jesus came that you might have life and have it more abundantly.

Satan's intention is to discourage, deter, and distract you. He takes pleasure in keeping you down. However, Jesus came that you may experience fullness of joy. He wants you to have live and have life more abundantly. In other words, He wants you not only to live but thrive! He wants you to know fully who you are and Whose you are so that you can walk in victory in every area of your life.

QUESTIONS TO PONDER

1) Does it feel like the Enemy has gotten the best of you? Explain.

2) How does knowing that Jesus came so that you may have life more abundantly make you feel about your circumstance? How can you begin to experience abundant life?

JOURNAL THE JOURNEY

_____

_____

_____

_____

_____

_____

_____

_____

_____

_____

_____

_____

_____

_____

_____

AFFIRMATION

Even when it does not appear to be so, I have the victory in every situation. Jesus has provided me life more abundantly.

13

A GREAT CLOUD OF WITNESSES

~

Therefore, since we are surrounded by such a great cloud of witnesses, let us throw off everything that hinders and the sin that so easily entangles. And let us run with perseverance the race marked out for us, ²fixing our eyes on Jesus, the pioneer and perfecter of faith... (Hebrews 12:1-2 NIV).

ON AUGUST 3, 1992, AS a cheering crowd looked on, while running the men's 400-meter run, Derek Redmond tore his hamstring at the 1992 Summer Olympics in Barcelona, Spain. Redmond's father, Jim, ran from the stands and brushed off security to join his injured son on the track. He put his arms around his son, and with tears in both their eyes, the father and son finished the race and made it to the finish line—together.

We too are in a race—the Christian race. The Hebrew

writer tells us to throw off every weight and sin that hinders us. What (or even who) is impeding, slowing down or blocking your progress in the race? What sin is slowing you down? Is God telling you to let it go? The writer continues this subject of focus and says that we are to run with perseverance, which requires keeping our eyes on the prize. Run the race with diligence.

Just like Redmond's race, a cloud of witnesses is also cheering us on, hoping we will keep the faith. We must also know that exactly like Redmond's father, who let nothing stop him from helping his son finish the race, our Heavenly Father is running beside us and at times, even carrying us victoriously to the finish line!

QUESTIONS TO PONDER

1) Can you recall a time when you have gotten tired in the race of life? What did you do?

2) What or who might you be running with or carrying that may be impeding your progress in the race of life? What steps will you take to finish the race strong?

Journal the Journey

_____

_____

_____

_____

_____

_____

_____

_____

_____

_____

_____

_____

Affirmation

There is a cloud of heavenly witnesses cheering me on in my walk of faith. I will fix my eyes on Jesus and persevere.

14

THREE TIPS
FOR EVERY BELIEVER

~

Be joyful in hope, patient in affliction, faithful in prayer
(Romans 12:12 NIV).

I F ANYONE CAN give us words of encouragement in times of difficulty, the apostle Paul certainly can. His life was filled with persecution, pain and adversity—all for the cause of Christ. He was falsely accused, beaten, imprisoned, stoned, shipwrecked, and faced so much more. Yet, his letters are full of encouragement, instructing believers to persevere. Romans 12:12 is no different.

Paul encourages the saints in Rome with the following words:

1) Be joyful in hope. The believer does not need to lose heart in midst of chaos, sorrow and difficult situations. Paul wants to remind believers that their emotional state is not based on what is, or what has happened to them. Rather, joy comes in knowing in Whom they have placed their hope—Je-

sus, the Christ, the hope of glory! When believers know and embrace this truth, they can have hope in any situation.

2) Be patient in affliction. Most of us want our trials to pass quickly. No one wants to endure pain over a long period of time, but Paul instructs us to be patient in tribulation. We are to rest in God and allow His grace to cover us. We must endeavor to grasp all the lessons that God wants us to learn in that season.

3) Be faithful in prayer. We are reminded again to pray without ceasing (1 Thessalonians 5:16). Our prayers enable us to collaborate and cooperate with God in establishing His will on earth and in our situation, as it has already been established in heaven.

Take these three tips to heart and watch God change things.

Questions to Ponder

1) Are you experiencing adversity? Explain. How has this devotional encouraged you?

2) This week journal how you will be joyful in hope, patient in affliction and faithful in prayer.

Journal the Journey

_____

_____

_____

_____

_____

_____

_____

_____

_____

_____

_____

_____

_____

Affirmation

In life's difficulties, I am joyful in hope, patient in affliction and faithful in prayer.

15

HEAVENLY FOCUSED

~

Set your affection on things above, not on things on the earth (Colossians 3:2 KJV).

W E LIVE IN a world that is full of distractions. Over the years, the technology that has brought many benefits also consumes copious amounts of our time. Life as we know it is getting busier and busier. People move at a much faster pace than 50 years ago. As a result, one of the greatest tasks we face in life is to keep our focus on the things of God and not be distracted by the things of this world. How do we achieve this?

Paul gives us the simple answer in Colossians 3:2, which says, *"Set your affection on things above...."* You can pass this test by loving God more than *anything*. This is not a cliché but must be lived out while being careful that we do not fall into the trap of loving the things that represent God more than God Himself.

We can find God placed on the back burner in many ways. We can allow reading the Word to become a source of *information* rather than *transformation*. We can make church a social gathering, rather than a worship experience. We can make prayer a ritual rather than a relationship.

To keep our affection on things above is to maintain our love, our attention, and our passion for God and not on those things that consume the world. You might ask, "Well, how do I know whether or not I have passed the test? How do I know whether my affection is on things above?"

Paul also provides the answer to this question. You will know that your affection is on things above when it is not focused on the things on the earth. In other words, you will know whether your affection is on the things above by your attitude regarding earth's abundance. In order to pass the test, we must loosely wear the garments of the world. Love God more than anything! I don't know about you, but this is one test I don't want to have to re-take. I want to pass the first time!

Questions to Ponder

1) What or who consumes most of your time? What or who is on your mind most of the time?

2) What steps will you take to ensure that you remain heavenly focused?

Journal the Journey

_____

_____

_____

_____

_____

_____

_____

_____

_____

_____

_____

_____

_____

Affirmation

I love the Lord with all my heart, soul and mind.

16

ROAD KILL

~

But Lot's wife looked back, and she became a pillar of salt (Genesis 19:26 NIV).

WHILE HURRIEDLY DRIVING to work one morning, a squirrel ran into the street directly in my path. I braced both my hands on the steering wheel, tapped my brakes and hoped for the best. I dared not swerve to the left or else I would have crashed into oncoming traffic. Making a mad dash to the right would have landed me in a ditch. As a result, I had no other recourse but to continue straight and hope the little guy would scurry on across the street. However, once he reached the middle of the road, he stopped! He appeared to be confused. He went forward a few steps but then with a look of indecision, and in a split second, he turned back. I closed my eyes (you heard me right—I closed my eyes) and continued to drive forward, only to hear a big "THUMP!" I looked in the rearview mirror and saw the squirrel lying lifeless in the middle of the road. I felt terrible. *If only he had kept going,* I thought. *If he hadn't turned back, he would still be alive.*

The same indecision is true of Lot's wife. She and Lot had been given instructions to leave the city of Sodom and Gomorrah because God was going to destroy the land. The Bible tells us as they were making their exit, Lot's wife looked back and turned into a pillar of salt. This story is an everlasting reminder that when God has given instructions and has promised deliverance, we are not to get in the middle of the road and become indecisive.

Sometimes attachments and indecision can cost you more than you will want to pay. My friend, move forward and don't go back lest you become road kill!

QUESTIONS TO PONDER

1) What decision has you standing indecisively in the middle of the road? Is it the fear of a lack of faith?

2) Is God perhaps challenging you to move forward?

JOURNAL THE JOURNEY

_____

_____

_____

_____

_____

_____

_____

_____

_____

_____

_____

_____

_____

AFFIRMATION

God has given me wisdom and discernment to make good decisions.

17

MIRACLES
IN THE MUNDANE

~

*When Jacob awoke from his sleep, he thought, "Surely the
LORD is in this place, and I was not aware of it"* (Genesis
28:16 NIV).

HAVE YOU EVER experienced a miracle? Many might
answer, "no" because they have never experienced
a miraculous healing, witnessed a lame person get out of a
wheelchair or gained the ability to see. However, I want to
tell you that you experience miracles every day. Sadly, many
people miss the divine intersection of the spirit realm that
causes a natural phenomenon because they are looking for
magic—not miracles.

We can get so caught up with the mundane routine of life
that it blinds us from seeing God's hand at work. God is at work
everywhere and at all times. Jacob had an extraordinary dream
in an ordinary place.

I challenge you to go about your daily routine looking for the miraculous. You will find that miracles are happening all around you. As you begin to experience miracles in the mundane, I pray you will able to say like Jacob, *"Surely the LORD is in this place, and I was not aware of it."*

QUESTIONS TO PONDER

1) What miracles have occurred your life that perhaps you discounted or even missed?

2) What steps will you take to intentionally look for God's miraculous work?

JOURNAL THE JOURNEY

_____

_____

_____

_____

_____

_____

_____

_____

_____

_____

_____

_____

_____

_____

_____

_____

_____

_____

_____

Affirmation

Today I will look for and witness miracles in the mundane!

18

LIVING BEYOND
YOUR CIRCUMSTANCES

~

We are troubled on every side, yet not distressed; we are perplexed, but not in despair; ⁹Persecuted, but not forsaken; cast down, but not destroyed (2 Corinthians 4:8-9 KJV).

As we read these words of Paul, we can attest that these verses indeed describe his personal testimony. If anyone knew what it meant to suffer for Christ, Paul did.

Perhaps you can identify with Paul. You may be experiencing trouble on every hand. You may feel as though everything is going wrong in your life. Perhaps you are perplexed, confused and bewildered. You may even feel cast down and tossed aside.

Paul gives every suffering Christian a word of hope, as he encourages us to live beyond our circumstances. This paradox that Paul writes under the influence of the Holy Spirit emphasizes that although the apostle was faced with many trials, he testified that he was not distressed, he was not in despair and he was not destroyed. In other words, Paul had learned to live beyond his circumstances.

You too can overcome your circumstances. Know that whatever you may be going through, God has given you what you need to transcend every situation. You can live beyond your circumstance—not in denial of reality, but in full awareness, yet living by faith and in the hope of Jesus Christ. Trust God in every circumstance, and He will give you the power to live beyond it!

QUESTIONS TO PONDER

1) Have you ever felt discouraged and wanted to give up? Explain.

2) How and why do you think Paul was able to transcend his circumstances? What will you do to begin living beyond your circumstances?

JOURNAL THE JOURNEY

_____

_____

_____

_____

_____

_____

_____

_____

_____

_____

_____

_____

_____

_____

Affirmation

God has given me the power to live beyond every difficult circumstance!

19

IN THE FATHER'S HANDS

~

But when she could hide him no longer, she got a papyrus basket for him and coated it with tar and pitch. Then she placed the child in it and put it among the reeds along the bank of the Nile (Exodus 2:3 NIV).

Do you know that God's plan cannot be thwarted? I was blessed by revisiting the story of Jochebed, the mother of Moses. She gave birth to Moses during the devastating time when Pharaoh had ordered the death of every male child. The mandate of this genocide was designed to stop the plan of God, but Jochebed was determined that her son would live. She protected him as long as she could, and when she couldn't any longer, she placed him in the hands of the Lord. Jochebed placed Moses in the Nile River—the same river where other children were dying.

However, Moses' outcome was different. He was saved from the dangers of the river and was given a wonderful life, nurtured and reared by his own mother at the request of the daughter of the one who had ordered his demise. This powerful message for all parents relates to rearing children. As parents, our job is to love our children. Additionally, we are their protectors. However, a time comes with most of our children that we have to let them go. The apron strings are to be cut. At this time we must remember they are in the hands of the Lord and His plan for them will prevail.

QUESTIONS TO PONDER

1) If you are a parent, write down some ways you have protected your child(ren). If you are not a parent, how have you felt the need to protect a dream? A relationship? A business? A project?

2) How have you had to trust God with your child(ren)? Your dream? Your relationship? Your business? Your project?

JOURNAL THE JOURNEY

_____

_____

_____

_____

_____

_____

_____

_____

_____

_____

_____

_____

_____

_____

_____

_____

_____

_____

Affirmation

I trust God with all that is important to me!

20

Just Go with the Flow

~

Many are the plans in a person's heart, but it is the Lord's purpose that prevails (Proverbs 19:21 NIV).

M
Y YOUNGEST DAUGHTER is a planner and an executer. Ever since she was a little girl, she had to know the game plan for all activities in advance. She wasn't satisfied unless she knew what we were getting ready to do, where we were going, when we would arrive and the schedule once we were there. I didn't like giving her the "play by play" because she would be upset if the plan encountered a detour. As she rode in the car, she would ask what seemed like 50 questions. "Mom, where are we going?" I'd answer her question, which would then lead to the next question, "Where are we going after that?"

After a series of questions, I found myself saying, "Destiny, just go with the flow!"

Perhaps you can attest to having been on the ride of life.

Perhaps in your desire to be successful, you made play-by-play plans, and you set goals. However, those plans and goals did not materialize exactly as you anticipated—not because they were bad but because God had another plan. Knowing that it is acceptable to make plans and set goals is important to grasp. Plans and goals infuse our lives with direction, focus and momentum. However, Scripture lets us know that God's plan is the one that will succeed. Go ahead and make plans and set goals, but when things don't go as planned, God may be telling you to "just go with the flow!"

QUESTIONS TO PONDER

1) What plans have you made in life? Did you consult God before making them?

2) Are you trusting God with your plans? How will you respond if God changes them?

JOURNAL THE JOURNEY

_____

_____

_____

_____

_____

_____

_____

_____

_____

_____

_____

_____

_____

_____

Affirmation

I trust God, and I know His plan is best for my life.

21

God Has a Plan

~

"For I know the plans I have for you," declares the LORD,
*"plans to prosper you and not to harm you, plans to give
you hope and a future"* (Jeremiah 29:11 NIV).

HAVE YOU EVER found yourself in a really hard place
in life? Perhaps you felt alone, away from the famil-
iar, isolated and even rejected. Such was the case with the Israelites in Jeremiah 29, as they found themselves in exile, held
in Babylonian captivity for 70 years. God basically told them
three hard facts:

First, know that I carried you into exile. If God carried you
into exile, He knows you are there and is in control while you
languish there.

Second, move forward while you are in exile. Jeremiah told
them to "live" while they were in exile. He instructed them to
"build houses, settle down, plant gardens, marry and seek the
peace of Jerusalem." In other words, don't give up and die in
exile, but keep moving forward.

Third, pray for your city of exile. God told them to pray

for the place and the people who were holding them captive. Praying for the Babylonian people brought them blessings, and when the Babylonians were blessed, the Israelites would also be blessed.

You must know that in the midst of your exile experience, God knows exactly where you are, and He is in control. Keep moving forward and choose to live. Remember to pray blessings for those around you because as they are blessed, you will also be blessed.

QUESTIONS TO PONDER

1) Who or what situation seems to be holding you hostage, stifling your growth or discouraging you?

2) How are you applying the three steps in this devotion? How are you reminding yourself that God knows where you are and is with you? How are you moving forward? Are you praying for those around you?

JOURNAL THE JOURNEY

_____

_____

_____

_____

_____

_____

_____

_____

_____

_____

_____

_____

_____

_____

_____

Affirmation

I know that God's plan for my life will prevail—no matter what!

22

God's Charge to You!

~

And what does the LORD require of you? To act justly and to love mercy and to walk humbly with your God (Micah 6:8b NIV).

POLICE BRUTALITY, CIVILIAN retaliation, terrorist attacks, political candidacy wars, and immorality are just a few of the realities of our world. How do we as believers respond? Do we simply continue with our lives, "business as usual"—as if nothing is going on? Do we turn our heads the other way? When we get through praising our God on Sunday, how do we encounter a lost world on Monday?

My heart grieves every time I hear of another needless tragedy. Yet, at the same time, God's Word would not be true if it were not happening. But what is the believer's responsibility?

In the midst of sin, disobedience and rebellion, God gave Israel instructions to *"act justly, love mercy and walk humbly with your God."* Those words ring loud and clear to us today. As you make decisions, encounter people, face difficult situations and go throughout your daily routine, God's charge to us is to treat people right, have compassion for others, and walk humbly with your God.

QUESTIONS TO PONDER

1) How has the ills of our society impacted you? What is your response?

2) What steps you will take going forward to respond to act justly, love mercy and humbly walk with God?

JOURNAL THE JOURNEY

_____

_____

_____

_____

_____

_____

_____

_____

_____

_____

_____

_____

_____

_____

_____

_____

_____

AFFIRMATION

God has given me the ability to act justly,
love mercy and to walk humbly before Him!

23

THE PEACE OF GOD

~

And the peace of God, which passeth all understanding, shall keep your hearts and minds through Christ Jesus (Philippians 4:7 KJV).

IF YOU HAVE accepted Jesus Christ as your personal Savior, you have made peace *with* God. You have been declared righteous, justified, and you now have eternal life. Although many believers have made *peace with God*, they do not experience the *peace of God* in their daily lives. They are confident that when they die, they will spend eternity in heaven; however, their days on earth are spent worrying and full of anxiety, fear, frustration, and anger. The list of negative emotions people embrace is endless.

The Bible reminds us that we don't have to worry about anything. When you feel yourself going down the track of worry, tell God about it. The Bible tells us that we can make every request known to Him (while thanking Him in the process). Receive the peace that only He can give. He will keep your heart and your mind through Christ Jesus (Philippians 4:6-7).

However, you must know that you can never have the peace *of* God if you have not made peace *with* God (salvation).

Perhaps you are reading this devotional, and you have not made peace with God and accepted Him as your personal Savior. You can do that right now by praying this prayer:

God, I confess that I am a sinner, and I know that salvation only comes through You. I am helpless to forgive my sins and save myself. I need a Savior. I believe that Jesus lived, and that He bore my sins when He died on the cross. I believe that Jesus was raised from the dead, which guarantees my own resurrection. I entrust my life to You. Come into my heart. I thank You that Your Word says, "If I confess with my mouth the Lord Jesus and believe in my heart that God raised Jesus from the dead, I am saved." Thank You for forgiving me of my sins and for saving me. Thank You for the assurance of salvation and eternal life. Thank
You for the Holy Spirit who will walk with me through every valley and empower me to grow and live in obedience to Your Word. In Jesus' name, Amen.

If you sincerely prayed that prayer, you are now saved and have made peace with God. Now that you have made peace with God, remember that when times get hard, you don't have to worry. Trust God. When you have made peace *with* God (salvation), you can have the peace *of* God (calmness of spirit) every day of your life.

Questions to Ponder

1) Have you made peace with God by asking Him to come into your heart? If not, what is stopping you from taking that step and making that decision?

2) If you have accepted Christ as your personal Savior and you are not experiencing the peace of God, what has you worried, afraid, or anxious? Try following these steps to help you begin to experience the peace of God.

- Find a Scripture that speaks to the situation about which you are worried.

- Find a quiet place to sit comfortably where you will not be interrupted.

- Pray. Tell God your concerns, your fears, and all that worries you or makes you feel fearful or apprehensive.

- Begin to thank Him for His provision, His mercy, His grace, for all that He has done.

- Read and meditate on the Scriptures you have searched for and found.

- Sit quietly for a few minutes. Do not get up immediately. Allow God time to speak. (Don't become discouraged if you do not hear His voice immediately or after following these steps once or twice. Remain consistent. You will be training your ear to listen and your spirit to calm your mind.

- Receive God's peace that is always available for you!

Journal the Journey

_____

_____

_____

_____

_____

_____

_____

_____

_____

_____

_____

_____

_____

_____

Affirmation

No matter what is going on in my life, I have the peace
of God every day because I have made peace with God.

24

SALVATION COMES
WITH AN EXPECTATION

~

So then, just as you received Christ Jesus as Lord, con-
tinue to live your lives in him, ⁷rooted and built up in
him, strengthened in the faith as you were taught, and
overflowing with thankfulness (Colossians 2:6-7 NIV).

I N THIS DEVOTIONAL, Paul lets us know that an expectation comes with our salvation. Conversion is the beginning of a lifelong relationship with God. E. Stanley Jones
writes, "Conversion is a gift and an achievement. It is the act of
a moment and the work of a lifetime." A wedding is the beginning of a lifelong committed relationship between two individ-
uals. They don't walk away after the wedding day, saying, "Well,
that's it. I've done my part." There is an expectation from that
day forward. They are expected to love one another, sacrifice
for one another, and work together to build a relationship that
pleases and brings glory to God. Likewise, Paul says, now that
you have received Christ, here is the expectation—continue to

live in Him, grow in Him, find strength in your faith and over-flow with thankfulness.

Salvation is an event, but spiritual growth is a journey. Our conversion, which brings us into a relationship with Jesus, comes with an expectation that we will continue to learn, grow and commit to the ways of God because of our love for Him. Remember, salvation is free and instantaneous, but it comes with the expectation of a continuous, ever-growing relationship with Jesus, which is the work of a lifetime.

QUESTIONS TO PONDER

1) Are you a Christian who accepted Christ, but one who has abandoned the relationship? Explain.

2) What steps will you take to continue to live in Him, be rooted and built up in Him, be strengthened in the faith as you were taught, and overflowing with thankfulness?

JOURNAL THE JOURNEY

_____

_____

_____

_____

_____

_____

_____

_____

_____

_____

_____

_____

_____

_____

AFFIRMATION

I am committed to continually growing in my relationship with Jesus through _____
(fill in the blank).

25

NOT FOR SALE

~

When Simon saw that the Spirit was given at the laying on of the apostle's hands, he offered them money ^{19}*and said, "Give me also this ability so that everyone on whom I lay my hands may receive the Holy Spirit"* (Acts 8:18-19 NIV).

WE LIVE IN a day and time when people think money can buy nearly anything. Yes, education provides opportunity and money provides exposure, but some things cannot be purchased or negotiated—no matter how much money you may have.

Such was the case with Simon the sorcerer (Acts 8) who witnessed the power of the Holy Spirit through the apostles in Samaria. He wanted what they had and erroneously thought it could be purchased. He offered them money, saying, "Give me this ability." However, anointing cannot be purchased. The Holy Spirit is not for sale!

The Holy Spirit is a gift that is given only through believing and receiving Jesus Christ. Ephesians 2:8 tells us that "we are saved by grace, through faith—not of ourselves, it is the gift of God." If you want God's power, put your money back in your pocket. It is free! You need only receive Jesus Christ as your Savior. How do you do this? It's simple, *"Confess with your mouth that Jesus is Lord and believe in your heart that God raised him from the dead, you will be saved"* (Romans 10:9b ESV).

QUESTIONS TO PONDER

1) Have you ever coveted the gifting or anointing you see in someone else's life? What was it about the person that attracted you?

2) Now that you understand that the power of the Holy Spirit cannot be obtained by your own means, what steps will you take to receive Jesus and the power of the Holy Spirit?

JOURNAL THE JOURNEY

_____

_____

_____

_____

_____

_____

_____

_____

_____

_____

_____

_____

_____

_____

Affirmation

Through Jesus Christ, I am filled with the power of the Holy Spirit!

26

POINTLESS BUSYNESS?
OR PURPOSEFUL BUSYNESS?

~

We are merely moving shadows, and all our busy rushing ends in nothing. We heap up wealth, not knowing who will spend it. ⁷And so, Lord, where do I put my hope? My only hope is in you (Psalm 39:6-7 NLT).

W E LIVE IN a world where busyness is revered and applauded. When we meet someone, one of the first questions that surfaces usually is, "What do you do for a living?" Certain assumptions and even biases are attached to people according to what they do. Not only does our culture thrive on *what* a person does but also on *how much* a person does.

The busier a person is, the more impressive it seems to be. Our society prizes on multitasking and busyness. The more you can pile on your plate, the more impressive it sounds. The question is who are we trying to impress? Our long list of involvements, responsibilities, titles and accomplishments can simply be the result of a chaotic life we have built for ourselves—a life that leads to stress, unhealthy living, and no boundaries.

We must ask ourselves, "Why am I doing what I'm doing?" "Does my busyness have eternal value?" Psalm 39:6 states, *"We are merely moving shadows, and all our busy rushing ends in nothing...."* The other day I saw a video of a toddler running and crying because she feared her own shadow that was following her. We all know that a shadow, which is merely a reflected image, is not real. The Psalmist says we are merely shadows, and all our busyness lead to nothing. What a travesty to live our whole lives running and rushing everywhere, and it all lead to nothing.

We never saw Jesus rushing anywhere. He moved about with purpose. The only way to guard against the temptation of busyness is to be intentional and purposeful in what we do with our time. Busyness will come in all of our lives and being busy is not necessarily wrong. We must ask ourselves some questions:

- "Is my busyness purposeful or is it pointless?"

- "Does what I'm doing have eternal value?"

- "Am I building a spiritual legacy that will last beyond my earthly life?"

I challenge you to assess your to-do list and live purposefully!

Questions to Ponder

1) Make a list of all the things you do, including your responsibilities, projects, committees, assignments,

etc. Determine which ones are pointless busyness and which ones are purposeful busyness.

2) What goals or purposeful assignments have you put on the back burner because your plate has been full of pointless busyness? What changes will you make to re-prioritize your time and begin to live with purpose?

JOURNAL THE JOURNEY

_____

_____

_____

_____

_____

_____

_____

_____

_____

_____

_____

_____

_____

_____

_____

_____

_____

_____

_____

_____

AFFIRMATION

I will guard against pointless busyness and live my life
with purpose!

27

MAY I WASH
YOUR FEET?

~

*Jesus knew that the Father had put all things under his
[Jesus'] power, and that he had come from God and was
returning to God; ⁴so he got up from the meal, took off
his outer clothing, and wrapped a towel around his waist
⁵...and began to wash his disciples' feet... (John 13:3-5).*

I DON'T KNOW about you, but I love getting a pedicure.
I know of nothing quite like sitting back, relaxing, and
having someone pamper your feet. In John 13:3-5, Jesus shows
us what a real pedicure looks like. As Jesus' time on earth was
coming to an end, but He had yet another lesson He wanted to
teach the disciples. This lesson would be taught, not by words,
but by demonstration. As they were waiting to eat, Jesus took
off His coat (outer clothing), wrapped a towel around His waist
and began to wash the disciples' feet.

I believe that we can all learn some lessons from Jesus' example of servitude.

- Serve your enemies. Jesus washed Judas Iscariot's feet, even though He knew Judas was plotting to betray him. A true test of being a servant is when we can serve those whom we know do not have our best interest at heart.

- You can serve without reservation when you know who you are and Whose you are. The verse says that Jesus knew the Father had sent Him, had given Him power and that He was going back to the Father. You can serve others without hesitancy when you know who you are in Christ and that you are on His assignment.

- Don't allow pride to prevent you from being served. Not only was Jesus demonstrating humility and ser-vanthood by washing the disciples' feet, but knowing they were worthy. In order for the disciples to allow Je-sus to wash their feet, they needed to display a sense of humility and submission. This demonstration is the reason for Jesus later saying, *"no servant is greater than his master, nor is a messenger greater than the one who sent him"* (John 13:16 NIV).

Questions to Ponder

1) Jesus left us a great example of what servant-leadership and humility looks like. What steps will you take this week to lead and serve like Jesus?

2) Are you usually the one serving and find it difficult to be served? How will you exemplify humility and allow others to serve you this week?

Journal the Journey

_____

_____

_____

_____

_____

_____

_____

_____

_____

_____

_____

Affirmation

I can serve other because I am a servant of God!

28

RESTORE ME

~

Restore to me the joy of your salvation and grant me a willing spirit, to sustain me (Psalm 51:12 NIV).

PERHAPS, LIKE THE psalmist, you too have prayed this prayer. At some point, we have all found ourselves in need of God's restoration in our lives. Two categories of people need to be restored. First, those of us who need rest require restoration because we have disregarded our limits. We are fatigued, drained, exhausted and just plain tired, usually because we have kept going and going in spite of being depleted. As a result, we find ourselves like Mary in Luke 10:38-42, frustrated, irritated and overwhelmed because of the unrealistic expectations we have placed upon ourselves.

Secondly, some of us need restoration because we need to repent for disobeying God. Like Jonah (Jonah 1-4), we have rebelled against God and have chosen to do things our own way rather than God's way. Perhaps what God told you to do seemed too hard, too impossible or you simply didn't want to do it. As a result, the consequences have been grave, including losing your joy. Now you are praying like the psalmist, *"Restore to me the joy of your salvation...."* God is a God of restoration, and He will restore to you the joy you had when you first came to know the Lord.

Whether you need to rest or repent, God is a God of restoration!

QUESTIONS TO PONDER

1) Have you disregarded limits in your life? What steps will you take this month to find rest and restoration in Jesus?

2) Is there sin in your life that has stolen your peace and contentment? Upon our confession, our God forgives and cleanses us from all unrighteousness (1 John 1:9). What sin do you need to confess to experience God's restoration?

JOURNAL THE JOURNEY

_____

_____

_____

_____

_____

_____

_____

_____

_____

_____

_____

_____

_____

_____

_____

_____

Affirmation

I serve a God of restoration!

29

But God!

~

But because of his great love for us, God, who is rich in mercy, ⁵made us alive with Christ even when we were dead in transgressions—it is by grace you have been saved (Ephesians 2:4-5 NIV).

Have you ever had a "but-God" moment? To me, a "but-God" moment is a time of reflection about something you did in the past that you know you should not have done, or you went someplace that you know you should not have gone, or perhaps you were with a person with whom you should not have been associating…and then you thought, "BUT GOD!" As you contemplated these thoughts, you realized God kept you, protected you, shielded you, and covered you while you were in the wrong place, with the wrong person, or doing the wrong thing.

Your testimony might go something like this: "I could have lost my life, but God…" "I could have gotten sick, but God…" "I could have gone to jail, but God…" I think all of us have had a "but-God!" moment.

Paul was reminding the Ephesians that they had once been dead in their transgressions and sins, *BUT GOD!* God had been faithful. He had loved them in spite of themselves. He saved them—not because they deserved it—but because of His grace. Like the Ephesians, while we were disobedient, following our own desires, and deserving the wrath of God, God loved us, had mercy on us, and saved us. I encourage you to reflect on from where God has brought you and how He has kept you—even when you didn't want to be kept. BUT GOD!

QUESTIONS TO PONDER

1) In what situation have you been, that now when you reflect on it, you know God was faithful and protected you?

2) Now that you understand how the grace of God has kept you in your predicament, how will you show your gratitude to God?

JOURNAL THE JOURNEY

_____

_____

_____

_____

_____

_____

_____

_____

_____

_____

_____

_____

_____

_____

_____

_____

AFFIRMATION

Because of God's faithfulness to me, I am faithful to Him!

30

BE A BLESSING
AND BE BLESSED

~

And my God will meet all your needs according to his glorious riches in Christ Jesus (Philippians 4:19 NIV).

"**A**ND MY GOD *will meet all your needs according to his glorious riches in Christ Jesus.*" We often hear this verse quoted as a reminder that God is our provider, and He will supply all of our needs. God's Word is true, and God is and will forever be our provider. After all, Matthew 6:26 tells us that if God takes care of the sparrow, He will certainly take care of His children. Your employer is a source of your provision, but God alone is *the* source. We must never confuse the two.

Upon further study of the context of Paul's words to the Philippians, we find that these words come on the heel of Paul's commendation to the Philippians for their generosity and liberality. They had been a giving and supportive people, and Paul was reminding them that, as a result of their being a blessing, they would be blessed. God would provide for their every need.

May you be reminded to always hold your hands open, ready to give and be a blessing to others. As a result, you can be assured that you will never lack for God will provide for your every need. To whom will you be a blessing today?

QUESTIONS TO PONDER

1) Would other people say you are a giver?

2) It has been said that God sends blessings to those through whom He can get a blessing. Choose three people you will be a blessing to this month.

JOURNAL THE JOURNEY

_____

_____

_____

_____

_____

_____

_____

_____

_____

_____

_____

_____

_____

_____

_____

_____

AFFIRMATION

Because God has blessed me, I will bless others!

Wanda Bolton Davis is also the author of

Victorious Disciples:
A Practical Guide
for Christian Discipleship and Mentoring

CONTACT INFORMATION:
info@victoriousdisciples.org